Sarah Mühlebach

MISSION MOON

An Illustrated Guide to Space Exploration

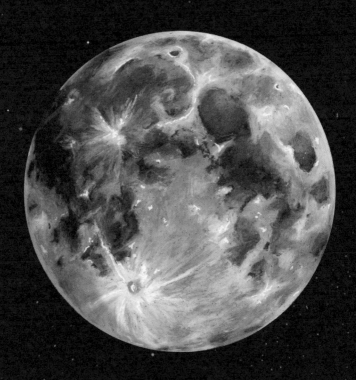

Translated from German by Marshall Yarbrough

HELVETIQ publishing is being supported by the Swiss Federal Office of Culture
with a structural grant for the years 2021–2025.

Mission Moon
An Illustrated Guide to Space Exploration

Originally published as:
3, 2, 1 ... Auf ins All!
Mit dem Mond auf den Spuren der Raumfahrt

Author and illustrator: Sarah Mühlebach
Typesetting and layout: Sarah Mühlebach and Ewelina Proczko
Translator: Marshall Yarbrough
Editor: Leah Witton
Scientific proofreader: Dr. Simon Christian Stähler, ETH Zurich
Proofreader: Angela Wade

ISBN: 978-3-03964-082-9
First edition: 2025
Deposit copy in Switzerland: March 2025
Printed in China

© 2025 HELVETIQ (Helvetiq AG)
Mittlere Strasse 4
4056 Basel
Switzerland

helvetiq.com

TABLE OF CONTENTS

In the beginning, there was just the Earth—and far, far away, the Moon.

On Earth, life emerged: tiny creatures at first, and over millions of years they grew bigger and bigger, and there were more and more of them, of all different kinds.

Some of them looked up and saw the Moon looking down at them.

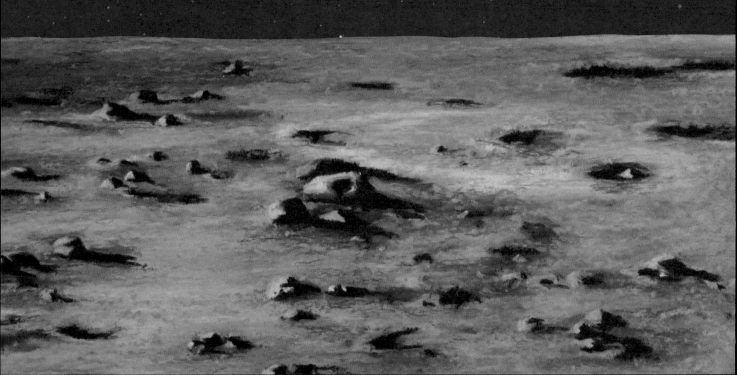

This is the story of our fascination with the Moon. It's a story of the questions humans have asked, and the journeys we have taken in search of answers.

The story of the exploration of space, and our study of the Moon.

The Earth and the Moon are inseparable. Earth's gravity keeps it from drifting into space . . .

. . . while the Moon's gravity is responsible for the ebb and flow of the tides on Earth, and explains the four seasons.

THE MOON AND THE EARTH

The Moon was once part of the Earth. It was formed 4.5 billion years ago from the blasted remains of material left over after a collision between Earth and another planet. Ever since then, the Moon and the Earth have influenced one another. The Moon's gravity attracts bodies of water on Earth and causes the tides. The same gravitational force keeps the tilt of the Earth stable on its journey around the Sun, which is why we have seasons.

Earth's inhabitants can feel the Moon's influence.

Flying foxes and bats are less active on nights when the Moon is full, because the extra light makes them more visible to their prey.

Once a year on Christmas Island, shortly after a full moon, **red crabs** make their way to the beach to mate and lay eggs. The ocean's current is weaker then, so the eggs don't get washed away.

GRAVITY

A strong force. Large objects like stars and planets exert a strong gravitational pull that acts like a giant magnet and attracts smaller objects. Gravity ensures that objects stay on the ground instead of just floating away, and that the Moon orbits the Earth.

The Moon's gaze is always fixed on the Earth . . .

. . . but the far side of the Moon—which people also call the dark side—is never visible from Earth.

LUNAR PHASES

Because the Moon takes the same amount of time to orbit the Earth once as it does to rotate on its own axis once, the side of the Moon that faces the Earth is always the same. How much of the Moon we see depends on how much sunlight falls on it.

During a **half moon,** half of the side that faces the Earth is lit up.

During a **full moon,** the whole side that faces Earth is lit up.

During a **new moon,** only the far side of the Moon is lit up, so we can't see the Moon from Earth.

The Moon's shadow can even darken the Sun.

During a **solar eclipse,** the Moon blocks the light of the Sun and casts a shadow on the Earth.

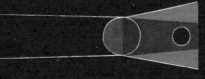

During a **lunar eclipse,** the Earth casts a shadow on the Moon.

During a lunar eclipse, the Moon often appears dark red.

SOLAR AND LUNAR ECLIPSES

Eclipses occur when the Sun, Moon and Earth are in a straight line. If the Moon is between the Sun and the Earth, there's a solar eclipse. If the Earth is between the Sun and the Moon, a lunar eclipse occurs.

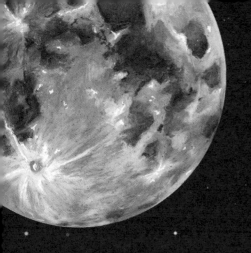

We call it the Moon, but for thousands of years, it had many other names, in many different languages.

CHANG'E (CHINA)

According to legend, Chang'e was once a woman. She drank an elixir and became immortal. Ever since then, she and her companion, the mythical jade rabbit, have watched over the Moon.

HANWI (NORTH AMERICA)

In the language of the Sioux, the name for the Moon translates to "night sun." Hanwi is said to protect us from evil spirits.

BAHLOO (AUSTRALIA)

Among Indigenous Australians, the Moon appears as an old man with white hair and three venomous snakes as pets.

CHANDRA (INDIA)

In Hinduism, Chandra is a young god who carries a mace in one hand and a lotus flower in the other.

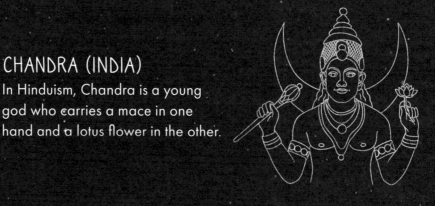

THOTH (EGYPT)

In the mythology of Ancient Egypt, Thoth was the god of the Moon, wisdom and magic. He was often depicted as a man with the head of an ibis.

MAMA KILLA (SOUTH AMERICA)

The Inca saw the Moon as a maternal figure. During lunar eclipses, they made noises to drive away the beasts that they believed would devour the Moon.

For many cultures the Moon served as a calendar . . .

. . . and people arranged their rituals and customs around its phases.

For the **Moon Festival**, which is celebrated in many Asian countries in fall, people light colored lanterns.

FESTIVALS AND TRADITIONS

The phases of the Moon are still important to many cultures today. In the traditional Chinese lunar calendar, the new moon determines when the new year begins. In Christianity, Easter is always celebrated on the Sunday after the first full moon in spring. The beginning of Ramadan, the Islamic month of fasting, is marked by the first appearance of the crescent moon after a new moon.

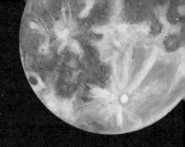

The invention of the telescope allowed people to study the Moon better than before . . .

. . . and they began to make drawings and maps of the Moon's surface.

EARLY ASTRONOMERS

A lot of what we know about our solar system today is based on the discoveries and theories of Galileo Galilei. He lived in the 17th century and studied the stars in the night sky with a telescope that he built himself. Based on his observations, he made detailed drawings of the Moon's surface. Galileo consulted texts written by Islamic astronomers from the Middle Ages, which were in turn built on even older texts from India, Persia and Ancient Greece.

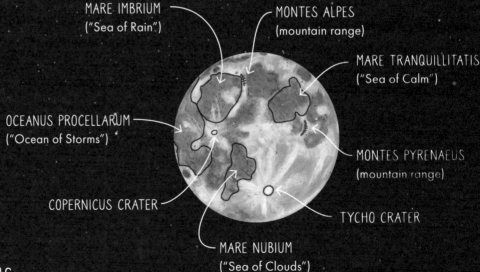

MARE IMBRIUM
("Sea of Rain")

MONTES ALPES
(mountain range)

MARE TRANQUILLITATIS
("Sea of Calm")

OCEANUS PROCELLARUM
("Ocean of Storms")

MONTES PYRENAEUS
(mountain range)

COPERNICUS CRATER

TYCHO CRATER

MARE NUBIUM
("Sea of Clouds")

SEAS AND MOUNTAINS

Mare, or *maria* in plural, is the Latin word for "sea." The large dark areas on the Moon are called maria because people used to think they were seas. The smaller, roundish spots are craters from meteorite impacts. The bright lines are mountain ranges.

At first, observations from Earth were
recorded with nothing but pen and paper . . .

The *Selenographia* map (1647)
by Johannes Hevelius showed
the Moon's surface in far greater
detail than earlier maps.

. . . then photographs were taken
with simple cameras . . .

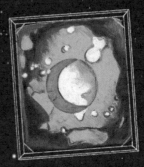

The oldest surviving photo of
the Moon was taken in 1840
by John William Draper.

. . . and, finally, probes were sent
into space to take photos.

In 1959, the lunar probe *Luna 3* took
the first-ever photo of the far side
of the Moon. Humans saw the dark
side for the first time.

LUNA 3
(Soviet lunar
probe)

UNIVERSE OR OUTER SPACE?
The Universe, also known as the cosmos, is an infinitely large
area that contains everything there is—all the stars, planets,
and moons—including our Earth. Outer space, or just space, is
the empty area (vacuum) between these planets and stars. The
invisible border between the Earth and outer space lies about
100 kilometers/62 miles above the Earth's surface.

For centuries, people had been thinking up tales of fantastic journeys—stories of adventurers who set out to visit the Moon . . .

Some traveled in ships that fell off the edge of the world . . .

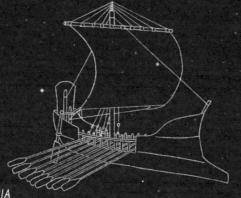

VERA HISTORIA
Story by Lucian of Samosata (2nd century)

. . . or with the help of birds . . .

THE MAN IN THE MOONE
Book by Francis Godwin (1638)

. . . and others in giant cannonballs . . .

. . . or with impressive rockets.

FROM THE EARTH TO THE MOON
Book by Jules Verne (1865)

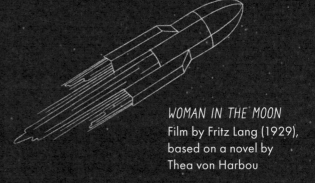

WOMAN IN THE MOON
Film by Fritz Lang (1929), based on a novel by Thea von Harbou

And then a new age dawned, in
which the fantastic tales that people
told became a reality.

The age of space travel had begun.

Humankind had a mission:
to journey to the Moon.

What's that gleaming in the
sunlight and orbiting the Earth,
just like the Moon?

A satellite! It's the first of its
kind, and just the beginning . . .

THE FIRST SATELLITES

The age of space travel began in the late 1950s with the building of the first satellites. Many more would follow in the years to come.

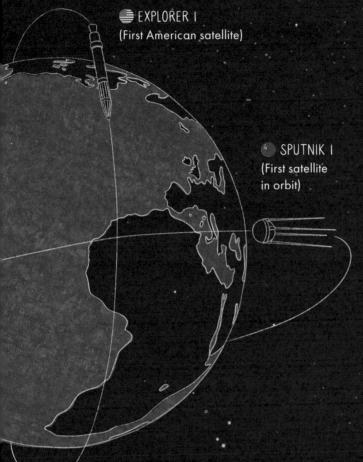

EXPLORER I
(First American satellite)

SPUTNIK I
(First satellite in orbit)

SPUTNIK I

On October 4, 1957, the first Soviet satellite, *Sputnik 1*, became the first human-made object to orbit the Earth. One complete trip around the Earth took about 90 minutes.

EXPLORER I

The first American satellite, *Explorer 1*, was launched on January 31, 1958. Its orbit was slightly higher than that of *Sputnik 1*, so it needed about two hours for one trip around the Earth.

The Soviet Union was able to maintain contact with *Sputnik 1* using ships that were equipped with radio receivers.

All the rockets in the bottom corners of the page are drawn to the same scale, so you can see how their size and shape have changed over the years.

ORBIT

In space, when gravity causes a smaller object to fly around a larger object, we say the smaller object is in orbit. When the Moon or a satellite makes one trip around the Earth, it has completed one orbit. The path it takes is also called its orbit.

R-7 (29 M/95 FT) - - - - - - - - - -
(USSR)

JUNO I (21 M/69 FT) - - - - - - - - - -
(USA)

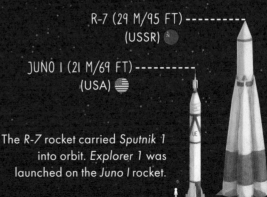

The *R-7* rocket carried *Sputnik 1* into orbit. *Explorer 1* was launched on the *Juno I* rocket.

Before people dared to travel to
space themselves, they sent other
inhabitants of Earth to the Moon.

Over the years, hundreds of animals
traveled to the Moon in tiny metal capsules.

Not all of them made it back to Earth.
Some remained in space, floating
among the twinkling stars.

ANIMALS IN SPACE

Before people flew to space themselves, they tested out their rockets
and space capsules using animals.

◗ HAM
(First hominid
in space)

◗ LAIKA
(First living
thing in orbit)

LAIKA

On November 3, 1957, Laika the dog
became the first living thing to fly in orbit
around the Earth. Unfortunately, she didn't
survive the flight.

HAM

Ham the chimpanzee became the first
hominid in space on January 31, 1961. After
the flight, he landed safely back on Earth.

Two dogs, **Belka** and **Strelka**, flew into orbit with other
animals in 1960 and were the first to land safely back on
Earth. One of Strelka's puppies was later given as a gift
to President John F. Kennedy.

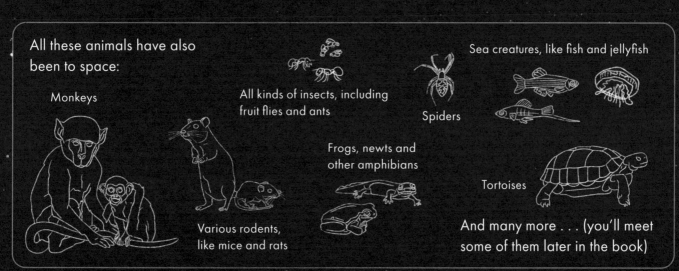

All these animals have also
been to space:

Monkeys

All kinds of insects, including
fruit flies and ants

Spiders

Sea creatures, like fish and jellyfish

Frogs, newts and
other amphibians

Various rodents,
like mice and rats

Tortoises

And many more . . . (you'll meet
some of them later in the book)

People on Earth grew restless.

Two powerful countries readied themselves. Both wanted to be the first to send a person into space.

Who would win the race?

THE SOVIET UNION

The Soviet Union's Vostok Program sent the first person into space.

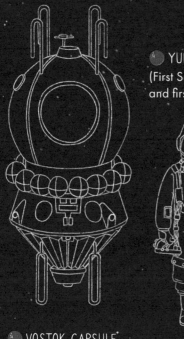

🌑 YURI GAGARIN
(First Soviet cosmonaut
and first person in space)

• MOSCOW

BAIKONUR COSMODROME
(Spaceport)

🌑 VOSTOK CAPSULE
(First Soviet space capsule)

SPACEPORT
A facility with several launch pads. This is where rockets are launched into space.

THE UNITED STATES

The first astronauts flew into space as part of Project Mercury.

WASHINGTON, D.C.

CAPE CANAVERAL
(Spaceport)

🌑 ALAN SHEPARD
(First American in space)

ASTRONAUT OR COSMONAUT
An astronaut is someone who travels to space.
In Russia, an astronaut is called a *cosmonaut*
(космонавт) and in China, a *taikonaut* (太空人).

🌑 MERCURY CAPSULE
(First American space capsule)

FREEDOM 7

THE FIRST PEOPLE IN SPACE

In the early 1960s, the first humans
flew into space and reached orbit.

YURI GAGARIN

On April 12, 1961, the cosmonaut Yuri
Gagarin became the first person to travel
to space. He orbited the Earth once, in
89 minutes, before landing.

JOHN GLENN

On February 20, 1962, John Glenn
became the first American to orbit the Earth.

YURI GAGARIN
(First cosmonaut and
first person in space)

JOHN GLENN
(First American in orbit)

Friendship 7

The name of John
Glenn's space capsule,
Friendship 7, was hand
painted on its side. Glenn
picked the name himself.

VALENTINA TERESHKOVA

On June 16, 1963, cosmonaut Valentina
Tereshkova became the first woman
to travel to space. She is also the only
woman ever to fly a solo space mission.

Another American, Alan Shepard, flew to space before John Glenn, but didn't orbit the Earth. The illustration below shows both missions, step by step.

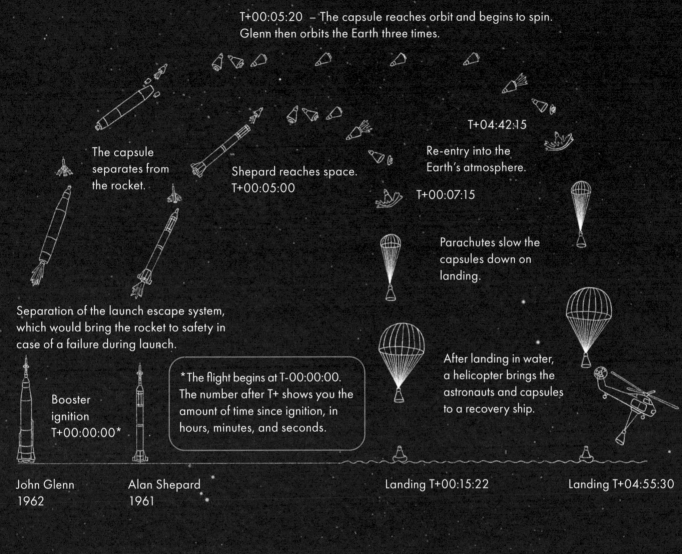

T+00:05:20 – The capsule reaches orbit and begins to spin. Glenn then orbits the Earth three times.

T+04:42:15

Re-entry into the Earth's atmosphere.

The capsule separates from the rocket.

Shepard reaches space. T+00:05:00

T+00:07:15

Parachutes slow the capsules down on landing.

Separation of the launch escape system, which would bring the rocket to safety in case of a failure during launch.

Booster ignition T+00:00:00*

*The flight begins at T-00:00:00. The number after T+ shows you the amount of time since ignition, in hours, minutes, and seconds.

After landing in water, a helicopter brings the astronauts and capsules to a recovery ship.

John Glenn 1962

Alan Shepard 1961

Landing T+00:15:22

Landing T+04:55:30

A farmer and her granddaughter saw Gagarin land. He greeted them with these words: "Don't be afraid, I am a Soviet like you, who has descended from space and I must find a telephone to call Moscow!"

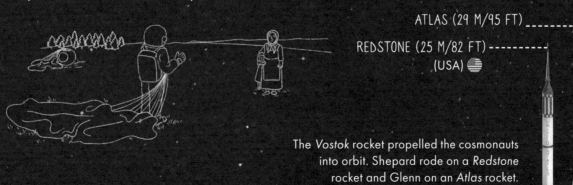

VOSTOK (38 M/125 FT) (USSR)

ATLAS (29 M/95 FT)

REDSTONE (25 M/82 FT) (USA)

The *Vostok* rocket propelled the cosmonauts into orbit. Shepard rode on a *Redstone* rocket and Glenn on an *Atlas* rocket.

The people who ventured into space attempted ever more daring feats. Some even climbed out of their capsules and floated in space.

From there, they could see the whole Earth, not just the small portion glimpsed through a tiny window.

ALEXEI LEONOV
(First spacewalker)

VOSKHOD CAPSULE
(Soviet space capsule)

SPACEWALKS

In 1965, astronauts and cosmonauts began to leave their
space capsules while in orbit and float freely in space.

ALEXEI LEONOV

On March 18, 1965, while orbiting the Earth,
Leonov left his space capsule and took the first ever
spacewalk. When he later became an artist, many
of his artworks were inspired by space.

EDWARD "ED" WHITE

On June 3, 1965, White became the
second person and the first American to
take a spacewalk. He floated in space for
roughly 20 minutes.

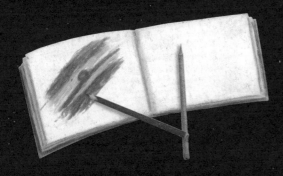

The **first drawing** in space was made
by Leonov after his spacewalk. It showed
the sunrise over the Earth. He'd taken a
sketchbook and colored pencils with him on
his mission.

VOSKHOD (44 M/I44 FT) ----------
(USSR)

TITAN 2 (33 M/I08 FT) ----------
(USA)

SPACEWALK

Whenever a person goes outside in space, it's
called a spacewalk. Of course, a person on a
spacewalk floats more than they walk.

The Soviet *Voskhod* rocket took
Leonov up into orbit, while White
rode on a *Titan 2*.

THE FIRST TRIP TO THE MOON

In 1968, the first astronauts flew to the Moon. They orbited the Moon and could see it up close for the first time.

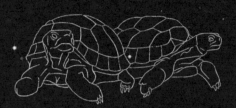

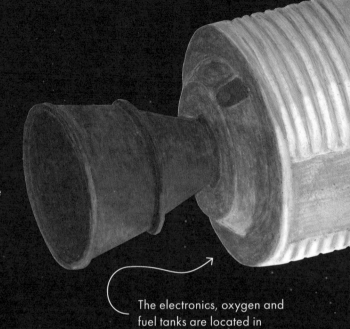

THE FIRST ANIMALS

On September 18, 1968, two tortoises completed one orbit of the Moon on the Soviet *Zond 5* spacecraft, becoming the first living things to fly to the Moon. The tortoises safely survived the week-long expedition.

The electronics, oxygen and fuel tanks are located in the service module.

THE FIRST PEOPLE

On the December 24, 1968, *Apollo 8* mission, Frank Borman, William Anders and Jim Lovell became the first people to orbit the Moon. They orbited it several times and were the first people to actually see the far side in person.

This photo, taken by William Anders, shows the Earth rising over the Moon. It bears the fitting title *Earthrise*.

JAMES "JIM" LOVELL 🇺🇸

Lovell is the only astronaut to fly to the Moon twice without landing on it. The first time was in 1968 with *Apollo 8* and the second time in May 1970 with *Apollo 13* (p. 28).

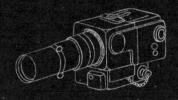

The astronauts took **cameras** and several rolls of film with them to document their missions.

APOLLO CAPSULE
(American space capsule)

The astronauts sit in
the command module.

They made it!
People had never
been so close to
the Moon before.

At this stage, they were
still only orbiting it but
that would soon change.

On Earth, three astronauts
were preparing to land on
the Moon and walk on its
surface for the first time.

THE MOON LANDING

In 1969, *Apollo 11* landed on the Moon—the first of the Apollo missions to do so. Five more Moon landings would follow over the next three years.

The upper edge of the flag is attached to a metal rod so that it can still 'flutter' even without wind.

"ONE SMALL STEP FOR [A] MAN, ONE GIANT LEAP FOR MANKIND."

🌐 NEIL ARMSTRONG
(First person to walk on the Moon)

🌐 BUZZ ALDRIN
(Second person on the Moon)

Neil Armstrong spoke these words on July 21, 1969, as he became the first person to walk on the Moon. Buzz Aldrin, the pilot of the lunar lander, followed him out. The two astronauts spent a little less than a day on the Moon, including two and a half hours outside the lander in special lunar spacesuits.

While on the Moon, the two astronauts received a phone call from President Nixon.

LUNAR LANDER
It takes astronauts from the space capsule in lunar orbit down to the surface. After the mission, the upper part of the lander can take off like a small rocket and fly back to the space capsule.

MICHAEL COLLINS 🇺🇸

Collins, the third astronaut making up the *Apollo 11* crew, stayed in lunar orbit and made sure that the lunar lander was able to dock with the space capsule on its return.

THE APOLLO SPACE CAPSULE

The space capsule is made up of three main parts: the lunar module, the command module, and the service module (see illustration on pp. 24–25). Two astronauts use the lunar module to land on the Moon, while the third pilots the command-and-service module in lunar orbit until they come back.

SATURN V (III M/364 FT) - - - - - - - - -
(USA) 🇺🇸

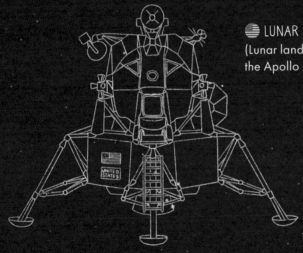

🌑 LUNAR MODULE
(Lunar lander for the Apollo missions)

The *Apollo 11* crew gave their lander the name *Eagle*.

SPACESUIT

Type of protective clothing that is made up of at least three parts: an airtight shell, under which space travelers wear cooling underwear; a helmet; and a suitcase or backpack containing oxygen. Depending on their purpose, spacesuits can have additional elements, like overshoes with rubber soles for walking on moondust.

All the Apollo missions were launched using a *Saturn V*, which at the time was the biggest rocket ever built.

THERE'S A FIRST TIME FOR EVERYTHING . . .

On later missions to the Moon, the astronauts did a few more things
for the first and, in some cases, the last time.

Apollo 13 (1970)
"HOUSTON, WE'VE HAD A PROBLEM."
After an explosion in the service module, a portion of the
capsule's fuel and oxygen supply was lost. The astronauts
couldn't fly directly back to Earth and they couldn't land on
the Moon either. They managed to return to Earth using a
risky maneuver that sent them careening around the Moon.

The movie *Apollo 13* (1995)
tells this story.

Apollo 14 (1971)
HITTING BALLS FOR "MILES AND MILES AND MILES"
Alan Shepard tucked a few golf balls and a golf club
in among the scientific instruments in his space capsule,
becoming the first and, so far, only person to play golf
on the Moon—although alone and without a hole.

The golf balls flew much farther
than they would have on Earth,
on account of the weaker gravity
on the Moon.

Apollo 15 (1971)
TIRE TRACKS IN THE DUST
On the last three Apollo missions, the astronauts took a
lunar rover with them. This **moon buggy** allowed the
astronauts to cover more ground and collect more rock
samples than on previous missions, when they had to travel
on foot. With the help of these samples, they were able to
study the Moon even better.

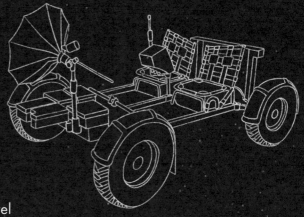

The lunar rover drove just
10 kilometers/6 miles per hour.

When the astronauts left the Moon to return home to Earth, all that remained were their tracks in the moondust.

People were soon hard at work on their next plan—building a space station. This would keep them busy for a while . . .

. . . but there was no doubt they would return to the Moon one day.

To date, the crew of *Apollo 17* (1972) are still the last people to have been on the Moon.

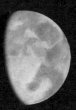

LABS IN ORBIT

In the 1970s, the first space stations were put into operation in Earth's orbit.

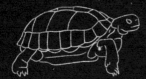

Tortoises spent almost 90 days on the Salyut 4 station. That's the record for the longest time spent by animals in space.

SVETLANA SAVITSKAYA

Savitskaya was the second woman in space. On July 25, 1984, she stepped outside the Salyut space station and became the first woman to spacewalk.

SPACE STATION

A scientific laboratory in space in which astronauts can live and work for several weeks or even months at a time.

SALYUT (1971–1986)

The first space station was the Soviet Salyut 1, launched in 1971. Between 1971 and 1986, further Salyuts were put into operation. Of the 48 cosmonauts who worked on the stations, ten were from non-Soviet countries, like East Germany or Cuba.

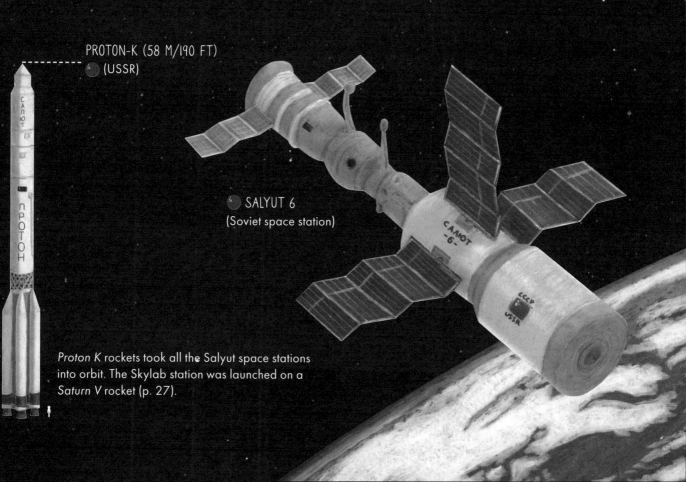

PROTON-K (58 M/190 FT)
(USSR)

SALYUT 6
(Soviet space station)

Proton K rockets took all the Salyut space stations into orbit. The Skylab station was launched on a *Saturn V* rocket (p. 27).

SKYLAB (1973-1974)

Skylab was the first American space station in orbit. Over three different missions, a total of nine astronauts spent 28, 59 and 84 days on the station, respectively.

Using triangular "cleats" on the front of their shoes, the astronauts could slot themselves into the triangular grid floor so they wouldn't float away while they worked.

On Skylab, the **spiders** Arabella and Anita proved they could spin webs in zero gravity. That same mission featured the first fish in space.

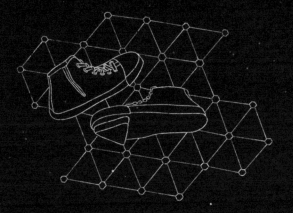

🌐 SKYLAB
(First American space station)

One of the two solar panels was torn off during the launch.

When they're no longer needed, space stations are usually brought into a controlled descent over the ocean and allowed to burn up in the atmosphere like shooting stars. Skylab, however, fell earlier than planned, and pieces of the wreckage fell on uninhabited land in Australia.

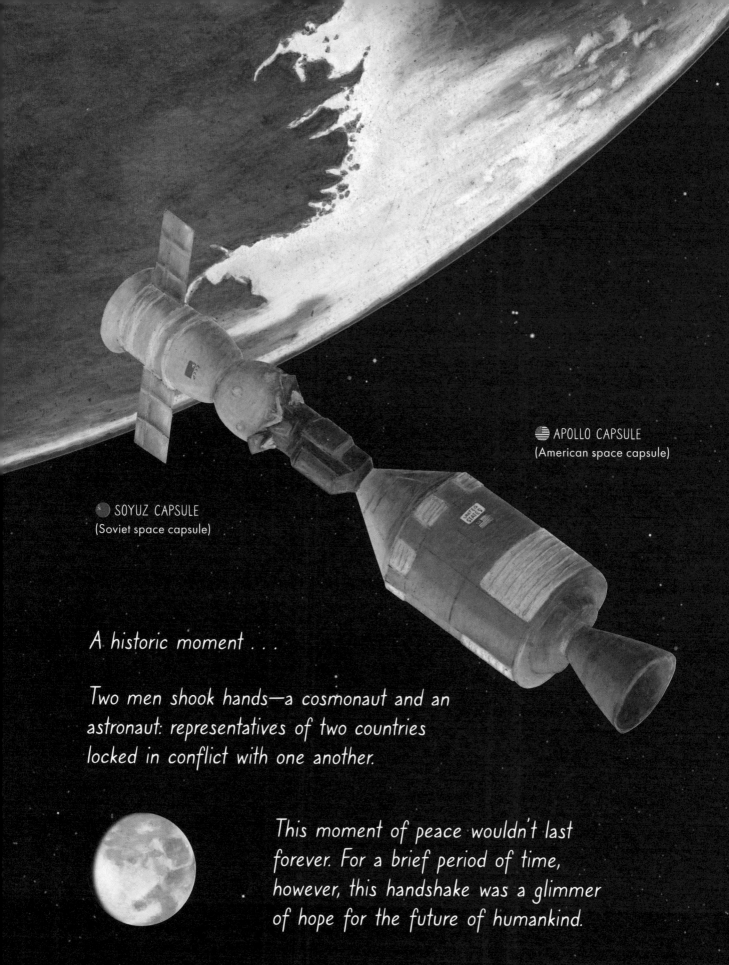

🌐 APOLLO CAPSULE
(American space capsule)

🌑 SOYUZ CAPSULE
(Soviet space capsule)

A historic moment . . .

Two men shook hands—a cosmonaut and an
astronaut: representatives of two countries
locked in conflict with one another.

This moment of peace wouldn't last
forever. For a brief period of time,
however, this handshake was a glimmer
of hope for the future of humankind.

A HANDSHAKE IN SPACE

In 1975, the United States and the Soviet Union worked together
on the Apollo—Soyuz Test Project.

HISTORIC HANDSHAKE

After years of competition, the USA and the Soviet Union
collaborated on the Apollo—Soyuz Test Project. This paved
the way for further international cooperation; like
the Shuttle—Mir Program (p. 40) or the International
Space Station (p. 43).

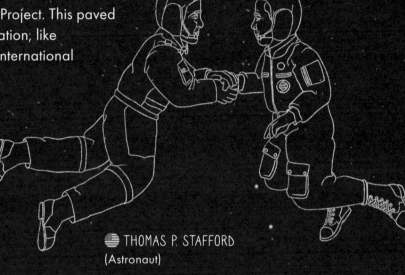

ALEXEI LEONOV
(Cosmonaut)

THOMAS P. STAFFORD
(Astronaut)

Soyuz—Apollo in Russian

СОЮЗ – АПОЛЛОН
APOLLO – SOYUZ

Apollo—Soyuz in English

SATURN IB (68 M/223 FT)
(USA)

SOYUZ-U (49 M/160 FT)
(USSR)

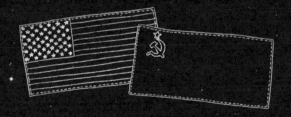

During the mission, the astronauts and
cosmonauts exchanged symbolic gifts,
such as their countries' flags.

The cosmonauts were launched into space
on a *Soyuz-U.* Seven hours later, the
astronauts followed them on a *Saturn 1B.*

THE SPACE SHUTTLE

NASA's space shuttles flew from 1981 to 2011.
They were the first partially reusable spaceships.

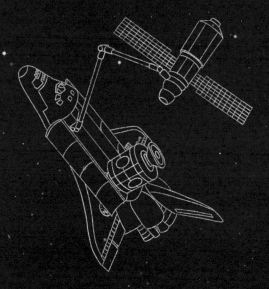

The space shuttle *Endeavour* secured the
first ISS module. Astronauts then went on a
spacewalk to connect it to the second module
they had brought with them.

LARGE PAYLOADS

With its 18-meter-/59-foot-long cargo bay, the
space shuttle could carry much larger and heavier
objects than rockets. Almost all the parts of the
International Space Station (ISS; p. 43), for example,
were carried into orbit by space shuttles. The shuttles
also had room for a crew of seven astronauts.

AFFORDABLE FLIGHTS?

The US wanted to make space travel less costly by
launching weekly space shuttle flights. In the end,
there were only three to five missions per year on
average, and they ended up costing a great deal
more than planned. By 2011, shuttles had flown a
total of 135 missions. That year, the program was
discontinued, in part because of the high costs.

---------- SPACE SHUTTLE STS (56 M/184 FT)
🌐 (USA)

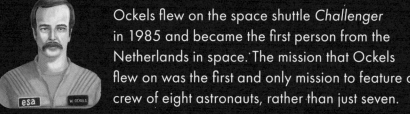

WUBBO OCKELS

Ockels flew on the space shuttle *Challenger*
in 1985 and became the first person from the
Netherlands in space. The mission that Ockels
flew on was the first and only mission to feature a
crew of eight astronauts, rather than just seven.

The Space Transportation System (STS) has several components, including an
orange fuel tank, two solid-fuel boosters—one on each side—and the orbiter,
of which five operational models were built: *Columbia, Challenger, Discovery,
Atlantis,* and *Endeavour.*

Then a new kind of spaceship began orbiting the Earth. These spaceships were much bigger than the previous small capsules.

🌐 BRUCE McCANDLESS II
(Astronaut)

COMPLETELY FREE

In 1984, Bruce McCandless II became the first person to float freely in space. No cable connected him to the space shuttle below. Instead, he had a special backpack, almost like a jetpack, that allowed him to fly around. This pack was called a Manned Maneuvering Unit.

🌐 CHALLENGER
(Space shuttle orbiter)

🌐 SALLY RIDE
(First female astronaut)

Thousands of young **jellyfish** helped scientists study the influence of weightlessness on our sense of direction. After a flight on the space shuttle *Columbia* in 1991, they had a harder time swimming than other jellyfish who hadn't been in space.

SALLY RIDE

Ride flew on the *Challenger* on June 18, 1983, and became the youngest American astronaut and first American woman in space. She is also the only known LGBTQIA+ astronaut to date.

RODOLFO NERI VELA 🪙

The only Mexican astronaut to date was also the first to take tortillas into space on a mission in 1985. They have since become a favorite space food for many astronauts.

🌐 HUBBLE
(Space telescope)

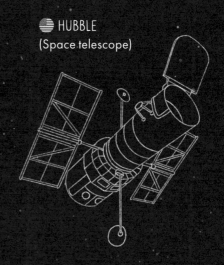

SPACE TELESCOPE

Telescopes on Earth have a limited range because of the atmosphere, which makes distant objects appear blurry, as if they were surrounded by fog. Space telescopes, because they are located outside the atmosphere, can capture much clearer images.

The **Hubble Space Telescope**, still active today, was taken into orbit in 1990 by the space shuttle *Discovery*. In 2021, it was joined by the James Webb Space Telescope, which provided even more detailed images.

A disaster awaited, but people on Earth didn't know it. Only few suspected that their efforts might end in tragedy, but even they couldn't prevent the catastrophe.

For months, people had been eagerly awaiting this launch . . .

Soon nothing would remain of the spaceship and its passengers but pieces of wreckage and the memory of soaring dreams.

The space shuttle *Challenger* disintegrated shortly after launch on January 28, 1986, due to material defects (p. 39).

FALLEN HEROES

These 21 astronauts and cosmonauts lost their lives on or in the lead-up to space missions.

VIRGIL "GUS" GRISSOM

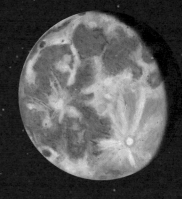

EDWARD "ED" WHITE   ROGER B. CHAFEE

APOLLO I (JANUARY 27, 1967)

The three astronauts died in a fire in the space capsule during a trial run that took place before the mission was launched.

Like some of the animals before them, some of the humans who boldly left Earth didn't make it back alive.

SOYUZ I (APRIL 24, 1967)

The space capsule's parachute failed to open upon re-entry and the capsule plummeted with nothing to slow its descent.

VLADIMIR KOMAROV

SOYUZ II (JUNE 30, 1971)

On re-entry into the atmosphere, a loose valve allowed air to escape from the space capsule. The three cosmonauts suffocated.

VIKTOR PATSAYEV   VLADISLAV VOLKOV   GEORGY DOBROVOLSKY

As the first teacher in space, McAuliffe was supposed to give a lesson during the mission.

CHRISTA McAULIFFE GREGORY JARVIS RONALD McNAIR

ELLISON ONIZUKA MICHAEL J. SMITH FRANCIS "DICK" SCOBEE JUDITH RESNIK

A soccer ball given to Onizuka by his daughter survived the explosion. Thirty years later, another astronaut took it with him to the ISS.

STS-51-L (JANUARY 28, 1986)

The space shuttle *Challenger* broke apart shortly after takeoff because of faulty seals in the rocket booster.

LAUREL CLARK WILLIAM C. McCOOL DAVID M. BROWN

Chawla was the first Indian-born woman in space and Ramon the first Israeli.

MICHAEL P. ANDERSON RICK HUSBAND KALPANA CHAWLA ILAN RAMON

STS-107 (FEBRUARY 1, 2003)

The space shuttle *Columbia* broke apart on re-entry, because of a damaged wing.

The Colombia Hills on Mars are a range of seven hills: each named after one of these seven astronauts.

THE MIR SPACE STATION

The Russian Mir space station, the first of the new, larger space stations,
was in operation from 1986 to 2000.

A space shuttle docks on Mir and allows astronauts to come on board.

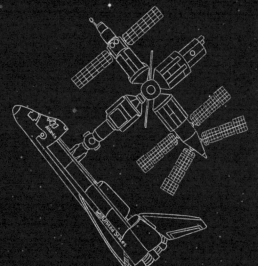

BUILDING IN SPACE

Unlike the Salyut and Skylab space stations (pp. 30–31), Mir wasn't launched into space as a single unit. Like the ISS (p. 43), it was made up of separate modules, each comprising a different part of the station, and assembled in orbit, one module at a time.

The **Shuttle–Mir Program** brought astronauts and cosmonauts together to fly on joint missions to the Mir space station.

TOYOHIRO AKIYAMA ●

Akiyama went to space in 1990, becoming the first Japanese astronaut and the first journalist in space. During his mission, he reported live from the Mir space station.

Akiyama took a few **Japanese tree frogs** with him to the space station.

STRANDED IN ORBIT

The cosmonaut Sergei Krikalev was on Mir at the time of the breakup of the Soviet Union. Since many of the Russian space agency's facilities were suddenly no longer on Russian territory, his return flight was delayed by several months.

SOVIET UNION (USSR)

Former country in Eastern Europe and Asia that was also known as the USSR. The Soviet Union was dissolved in 1991 and divided into 15 separate countries, including Russia, Ukraine and Uzbekistan.

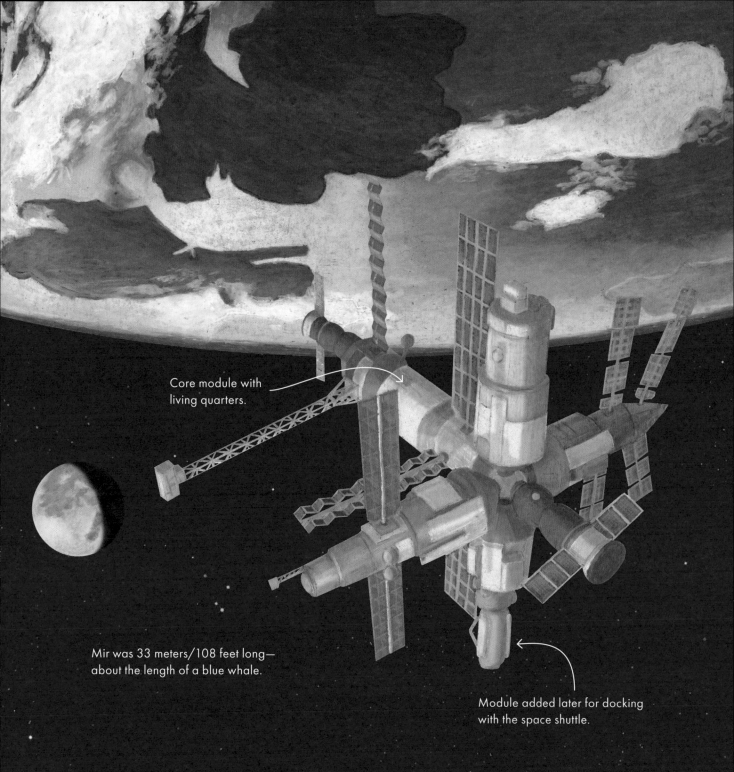

Core module with
living quarters.

Mir was 33 meters/108 feet long—
about the length of a blue whale.

Module added later for docking
with the space shuttle.

More and more space stations started circling the Earth,
and they were becoming even bigger and more complex.

But the biggest of them all—the space station that outshone
all its predecessors—was only just being built.

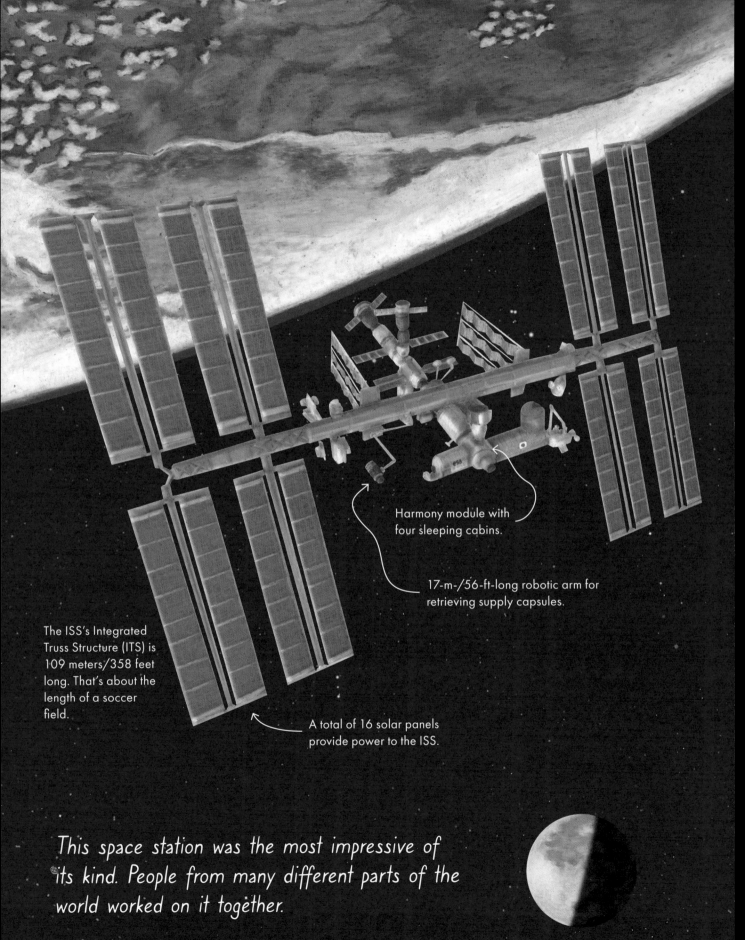

Harmony module with four sleeping cabins.

17-m-/56-ft-long robotic arm for retrieving supply capsules.

The ISS's Integrated Truss Structure (ITS) is 109 meters/358 feet long. That's about the length of a soccer field.

A total of 16 solar panels provide power to the ISS.

This space station was the most impressive of its kind. People from many different parts of the world worked on it together.

THE INTERNATIONAL SPACE STATION

The International Space Station, ISS for short, is the largest
human-built object in space.

In the early morning or late evening,
the ISS is sometimes visible as a bright
point moving across the horizon.

FLOATING CHAOS

To prevent objects in the space station from floating
freely in zero gravity, they have to be secured in
place. There are various fixtures and devices on the
space station for this purpose.

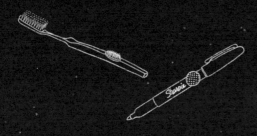

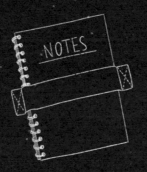

Objects like notebooks can
be held in place under **elastic
bands** mounted on walls and
surfaces.

Small objects like pencils and toothbrushes have
Velcro patches for sticking onto one of the many
Velcro strips that are found throughout the space
station—even on the pants the astronauts wear.

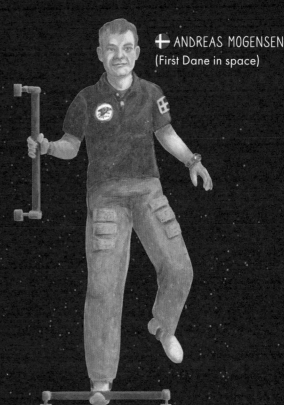

✚ ANDREAS MOGENSEN
(First Dane in space)

Handles allow astronauts to move around
the station more easily. If they want to stay
in one place, they can hook their feet under
one of the handles.

WEIGHTLESSNESS

Without gravity, everything on Earth would float
around as if it were "weightless." Although the ISS
is effected by the Earth's gravity, it's also being
pushed away by centrifugal force. This creates a
state of weightlessness in and around the station
that is sometimes called "zero gravity," even though
gravity is still technically present.

Elastic bands attached to the
cuffs of astronauts' pants keep
them from riding up.

NASA

National Aeronautics and Space Administration

Canadian Space Agency –
Agence spatiale canadienne

European Space Agency

Russian Space Agency

ROSCOSMOS

Japanese Aerospace
Exploration Agency

INTERNATIONAL CONTRIBUTIONS

Fifteen countries and five space agencies (listed on the left) are partners in the International Space Station. As of 2024, more than 280 people from more than 25 countries had worked on the space station.

SAMANTHA CRISTOFORETTI

In 2014, Cristoforetti became the first Italian woman in space. In 2022, she became the first European woman to command the International Space Station.

ESA

The European Space Agency, ESA for short, is a European partnership in which 22 countries are currently participating.

ARIANE 5 (59 M/154 FT)
(France, ESA)

Can you identify all the ESA member countries by their flags?

Ariane 5, ESA's most powerful rocket, was in operation until 2023. It was only equipped for uncrewed flights.

SAMANTHA CRISTOFORETTI
(First female Italian astronaut)

OVERVIEW EFFECT

Many astronauts who have gazed down at Earth from space have described the "overview effect." They see the Earth as a whole because when it is seen from above, no borders are visible. They see our planet's beauty and understand how important it is to protect it.

DAILY LIFE ON THE ISS

There are many things to do and see for astronauts
on the International Space Station.

WORK

Astronauts spend most of the day working.
They conduct scientific experiments, perform
maintenance on the station, or shoot videos to
explain their work to people on Earth.

On spacewalks,
astronauts make repairs
or install new parts.

THOMAS PESQUET
(French astronaut)

A few plants have successfully
been grown on the ISS,
including a small pepper plant.

EXPERIMENTS

Astronauts conduct different kinds of experiments:
to investigate the effects of weightlessness on their
bodies, for example, or to test ways to grow plants
on the space station.

In zero gravity, there is no weight on the
spinal column, so bones aren't pressed as
closely together as on Earth. On extended
stays in space, astronauts can grow up to
5 centimeters/2 inches taller.

— — 5'10.5"

— 5'8.5"

More blood collects in the brain in zero
gravity. The increased pressure on the
optic nerve worsens astronauts' vision.

Astronauts with long hair usually tie it up, otherwise it floats in all directions.

BATHING

Water is a scarce resource on the space station, so all liquids, including sweat and urine, are collected, purified and recycled as fresh water that the astronauts use for drinking and washing.

⊕ YI SO-YEON
(First South Korean in space)

Hair is washed with a dry shampoo that can be used with very little water.

CLEANING

Astronauts must regularly tidy up and clean the space station, because dust and dirt get everywhere in zero gravity and can clog up important instruments. So every Saturday on the ISS is a cleaning and tidying day.

Because there are no showers on the ISS, astronauts wash themselves with damp towels and soap.

To pee, astronauts use a funnel attached to a hose, which sucks up the urine and collects it for recycling.

TOILETS

There are three bathrooms on the ISS, each with two different devices that were specially developed for space.

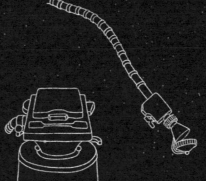

To poop, astronauts use a toilet with a seat and a seatbelt. The poop is collected in containers, which are disposed of in empty supply capsules.

FREE TIME

At the end of the workday, astronauts have a little time to themselves to call their families, enjoy the view or pursue their hobbies.

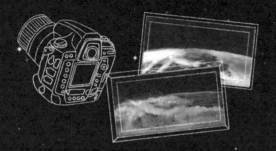

The Cupola (p. 45) is the Italian observation module. Astronauts can view Earth and take photos through its large windows.

CHRIS HADFIELD
(Canadian astronaut)

Some astronauts take musical instruments with them to the station.

US astronaut Karen Nyberg knitted a plush dinosaur toy out of old material while on the ISS.

TIMOTHY "TIM" PEAKE
(British astronaut)

Peake took part in the 2016 London marathon while on the ISS. He used elastic bands to secure himself to the floor and keep his feet on the treadmill. In 2007, the American Sunita Williams ran the Boston Marathon in the same way.

EXERCISING

Spending an extended amount of time in zero gravity weakens the body. To maintain their strength, astronauts have to exercise daily on specially built exercise machines.

◗ KŌICHI WAKATA
(Japanese astronaut)

It's bright and loud on the space station, like on a plane. Sleeping pills, ear plugs and masks help astronauts sleep.

SLEEPING

The sleeping cabins on the ISS have just enough room for a sleeping bag, a laptop, and a few personal items.

The sleeping bags are secured to the wall so the astronauts don't float around in their sleep.

EATING AND DRINKING

Astronauts get to plan the meals they'll eat on their mission themselves. The meals are then prepared and processed to last. On the ISS, they can be prepared by adding water or warming them up in the oven.

◗ ALEXANDER GERST
(German astronaut)

Astronauts on the ISS drink out of pouches with straws that look a little bit like space Capri-Suns.

Meals are usually eaten directly out of the pouches or cans that the food was warmed up in.

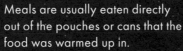

Supply capsules regularly bring fresh fruit and vegetables as well as sweets to the space station.

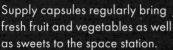

Because of zero gravity, astronauts always have stuffy noses. As a result, their food has less taste, kind of like when you have a cold. Because of this, spicy food, like this taco with peppers grown on the station, is especially well liked.

THE TIANGONG SPACE STATION

China's Tiangong space station has been in operation since 2021 and
like the ISS (p. 43) and Mir (p. 40) is made up of several modules.

LIU YANG

Yang became the first female taikonaut in
2012, nine years after Yang Liwei became
the first Chinese person in orbit. In 2022,
Liu Yang flew to the Tiangong space station.

At first, China had two smaller
space stations, Tiangong 1 and
Tiangong 2, which in shape
and size resembled Salyut and
Skylab (pp. 30-31).

CHINA

China launched its first satellites in 1970. Today, it has the world's
fourth-largest space program, behind Russia, the USA and ESA.

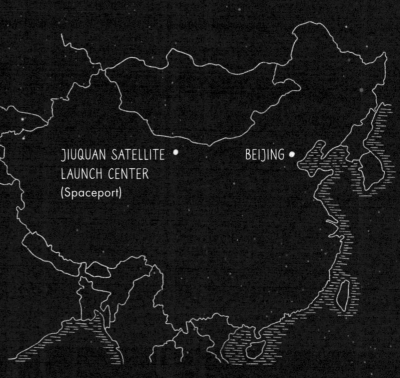

CHANG ZHENG 2F (62 M/203 FT)
(China)

JIUQUAN SATELLITE
LAUNCH CENTER
(Spaceport)

BEIJING

*Chang Zheng 2F, which means "Long
March 2F" in English, is China's only
rocket for crewed spaceflights.*

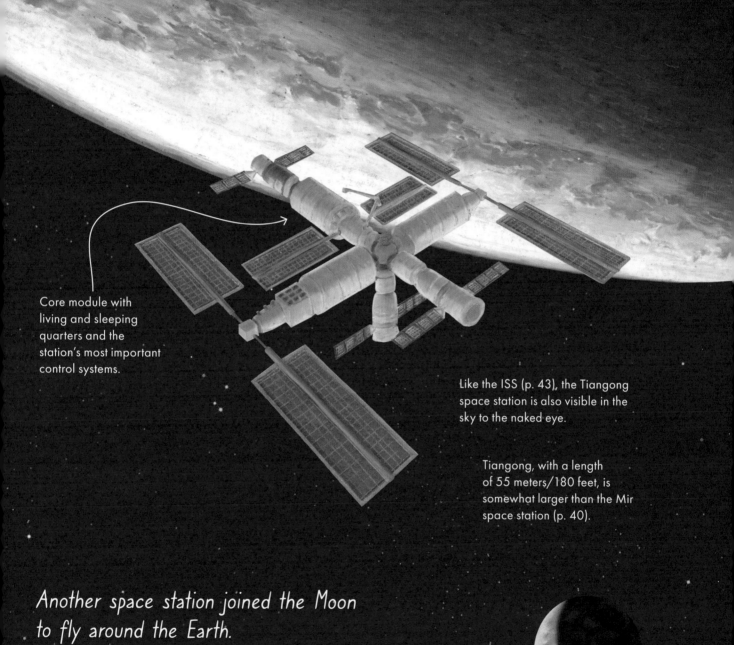

Core module with
living and sleeping
quarters and the
station's most important
control systems.

Like the ISS (p. 43), the Tiangong
space station is also visible in the
sky to the naked eye.

Tiangong, with a length
of 55 meters/180 feet, is
somewhat larger than the Mir
space station (p. 40).

Another space station joined the Moon
to fly around the Earth.

Its name means "heavenly palace"
in the language of its builders.

Alongside human-made satellites and space stations, the Moon is joined by other objects.

There are many small pieces of rock that fly through space and are sometimes captured by the Earth's gravitational pull.

QUASI-SATELLITES

Earth has several so-called "quasi-satellites." These are asteroids that accompany the Earth in its orbit around the Sun. The quasi-satellite *Kamo'oalewa*, discovered in 2016, has accompanied the Earth for more than 100 years and is probably a part of the Moon that split off after a meteorite impact.

ASTEROIDS, METEOROIDS & CO.

There are many objects in space that are smaller
than planets and moons.

ASTEROIDS

Asteroids are chunks of rock and metal that fly
through space. Some of them are more than a
hundred miles wide.

METEOROID

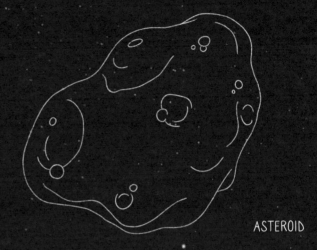

ASTEROID

A **meteoroid** is a small
asteroid, with a diameter of
only a few feet.

METEORITE

A **meteor** is a streak of light that occurs when
a meteoroid enters the Earth's atmosphere and
burns up. Meteors are also called shooting stars
or bolides.

METEOR

A **meteorite** is a meteoroid or asteroid that falls to
Earth. The crater that its impact causes can be over
one hundred miles wide, but most meteorites are
very small and only produce small craters, if at all.

COMET

COMETS

Comets are similar to asteroids but are not
just made of rock and metal but also of large
amounts of ice and various gases. Thanks to their
bright tails, which can be several hundred million
miles long, they can sometimes be seen in the
night sky with the naked eye.

In our solar system there are almost 300 moons that we know of. But there are probably many more that haven't been discovered yet.

EARTH

VENUS

Other moons are scattered all over the solar system and orbit other planets.

MERCURY

EARTH'S MOON

Some planets have no moons of their own . . .

. . . while others have so many that people keep discovering new ones.

SATURN

Mercury and Venus have no moons. Saturn, with more than 140 known moons, has the most of any planet in the solar system. One of them is Titan, the only moon we know of with its own atmosphere.

ENCELADUS

NEPTUNE

FENRIR

TITAN

There are large moons . . .

The largest moon in the solar system is
Ganymede, a moon of Jupiter, with a
diameter of 5262 kilometers/3270 miles.
Although our moon is smaller, it is one
quarter the size of Earth, which makes it the
largest moon relative to the size of its planet.

JUPITER

GANYMEDE

. . . and small moons.

MARS

Deimos, a moon of Mars, is only
15 kilometers/9 miles in diameter.
Some moons of Saturn are even
smaller, like Fenrir, which is only
4 kilometers/2 miles in diameter.

IO

DEIMOS

On some of them it's
scorching hot . . .

EUROPA

. . . on others it's icy cold.

On Triton, an icy moon of Neptune, the average temperature is
-235°C/-391°F. By contrast, it's really hot in the volcanoes of Jupiter's moon
Io, where temperatures of over 1500°C/2732°F have been measured.

And on some of them, there
could even be life.

TRITON

Saturn's moon Enceladus and Jupiter's moon Europa both have
liquid water under their ice-covered surfaces. Because they're so
far away, it's difficult to study them, but scientists hypothesize that
microorganisms—tiny living things like bacteria—could live there.

These planets and moons are not drawn to scale.

THE GRAND PLANETARY TOUR

In the 1970s, the United States sent space probes to the outer planets of our solar system in order to study them and their moons.

A LONG JOURNEY

The two *Voyager* planetary probes began to study the outer planets in 1977 and are still active today. Since 2012, *Voyager 1* has been sending back data about the universe outside our solar system. It has traveled farther from Earth than any other human-built object.

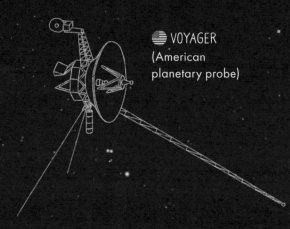

🔘 VOYAGER
(American planetary probe)

THE SUN
Yellow dwarf star

The illustration below and on the next page shows the different paths of the *Voyager 1* (V1) and *Voyager 2* (V2) probes on their journey through our solar system.

SATURN
Gas giant
V1: 1980
V2: 1981

MERCURY
Rocky planet

JUPITER
Gas giant
V1: 1979
V2: 1979

After Saturn, the paths of the two probes diverged. *Voyager 1* no longer flew close enough to a planet to be able to study it.

VENUS
Rocky planet

MARS
Rocky planet

EARTH
Rocky planet
V1: 1977 launch
V2: 1977 launch

CERES
Dwarf planet

These planets are not drawn to scale.

(EXTRA)TERRESTRIAL MESSAGES

The *Voyager* probes carry messages pressed on **golden records** in case they are found in the distant future by extraterrestrial life forms somewhere in the universe. In addition to a map of the solar system, they contain greetings in more than 50 languages as well as music, sound recordings and images of Earth.

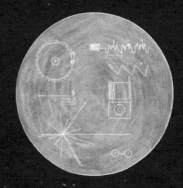

"GOLDEN RECORD"

PLANETARY RINGS

Planetary rings are made of chunks of ice and stone that orbit a planet. The rings of Saturn are particularly distinctive and were discovered quite early on. Others are less prominent, and were detected and explored for the first time thanks to the *Voyager* probes.

URANUS
Ice giant
V2: 1986

NEPTUNE
Ice giant
V2: 1989

Do you know the order of the eight main planets, starting with the one closest to the Sun? This sentence will help you remember:

My (**M**ercury)
Very (**V**enus)
Educated (**E**arth)
Mother (**M**ars)
Just (**J**upiter)
Served (**S**aturn)
Us (**U**ranus)
Nachos (**N**eptune)

Since 2006, Pluto is no longer classified as a planet, but rather as a **dwarf planet**.

PLUTO
Dwarf planet

HAUMEA
Dwarf planet

MAKEMAKE
Dwarf planet

ERIS
Dwarf planet

COMMERCIAL SPACE TRAVEL

In addition to state-run space agencies like NASA or ESA, there are also a growing number of private aerospace companies.

FAMOUS PASSENGERS

With its *New Shepard* rocket, the Blue Origin company has already sent a few celebrities into space. Among them are the actor William Shatner, the pilot Wally Funk, and Laura Shepard Churchley, the daughter of Alan Shepard (p. 19).

William Shatner, who played Captain Kirk in the science fiction TV series *Star Trek*, was 90 years old when he went to space, making him the oldest person so far.

Wally Funk went to space in 2021 as the sole representative of the "Mercury 13." They were a group of 13 women who underwent screening for the Mercury missions in the early 1960s but never took part in them.

FALCON 9 (70 M/229 FT)
🇺🇸 (USA, SpaceX)

DENNIS TITO 🇺🇸

The American businessman Dennis Tito flew on a Russian mission to the ISS in 2001 and stayed there for a week-long vacation. He was the first space tourist.

BLUE ORIGIN

Currently, the two largest private aerospace companies are the American SpaceX and Blue Origin.

NEW SHEPARD (18 M/60 FT)
🇺🇸 (USA, Blue Origin)

Falcon 9 regularly takes astronauts to the ISS. The smaller *New Shepard* rocket takes tourists into space, but not into orbit. *Falcon 9* is partly reusable and *New Shepard* is fully reusable.

FOR A GOOD CAUSE

In 2021, the American Hayley Arceneaux became the first person to travel to space with a prosthetic. She had bone cancer as a child and had to have her thigh bone replaced. She used her flight to raise money for children's cancer research.

STARSHIP (121 M/398 FT) ----------
(USA, SpaceX) ◐

PEGGY WHITSON ◐

Whitson holds several records, including for the longest total amount of time spent by an American in space. In 2023, she flew a private SpaceX mission to the ISS.

◐ CREW DRAGON ·
(SpaceX space capsule)

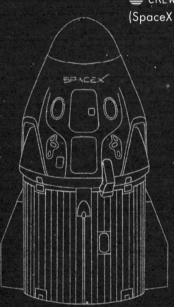

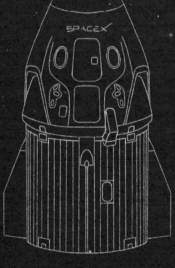

MOON CRUISE

SpaceX's *Starship* rocket is still in the test phase. It is the largest and most powerful rocket ever built—able to carry up to 100 passengers on a trip around the Moon, kind of like a cruise ship.

SpaceX works in partnership with NASA. Since 2020, its *Crew Dragon* space capsules have regularly ferried astronauts to the ISS.

Starship is supposed to be the first completely reusable orbital rocket (a rocket that flies into orbit).

Almost 70 years ago, the Moon
was joined by the first of many
satellites built by humans.

Now there are millions of objects—some small,
some large—floating around the Earth.

Most are debris that were
left in orbit.

CHAOS IN ORBIT

Today, there are so many objects in Earth's orbit that there is
a constant risk of collisions.

SPACE JUNK

Of the more than 10,000 satellites in orbit, several thousand are
inactive and are flying uncontrolled around the Earth. Added to
this are the discarded parts of rockets and space capsules. Space
junk flies through space at up to 28,000 kilometers/16,156 miles
per hour, and often satellites and even space stations have to
move out of the way. Collisions could result in severe damage
and scatter even more debris into space.

🌐 SLING-SAT
(American waste-
removal satellite)

WASTE REMOVAL IN SPACE

The goal for the future is to avoid generating any more
space junk. There are already a few ideas on how to
clean up the Earth's orbit, because the more debris there
is in space, the more dangerous it becomes to travel there.

Acting like a slingshot, the **Sling-Sat**
could fling smaller debris down to
Earth, where they would burn up in
the atmosphere.

🏴 REMOVEDEBRIS
(British waste-
removal satellite)

The **RemoveDEBRIS** satellite could retrieve
damaged satellites and larger debris using a
net or a harpoon and pull them towards the
Earth. There, both objects—the junk and the
junk collector—would burn up.

A long time after the Moon landings,
people are again sending objects there.

Small metal creations are orbiting
and landing on the Moon.

Very soon, people will follow them, and
this time they will be coming to stay.

A new, exciting chapter in the
Moon's history and the history of
humankind is about to begin.

In 2019, the Chinese lunar rover *Yutu-2*
was the first object to land on the far
side of the Moon.

YUTU-2
(Chinese
lunar rover)

🌓 🇮🇱 HELGA
(Dummy with
sensors)

Members of the *Artemis 1* crew
included NASA astronaut Snoopy
and ESA astronaut Shaun the Sheep.

Two **test dummies,** built to resemble female torsos, orbited the Moon in 2022
on *Artemis 1*. Equipped with sensors, they measured the radiation that a body
is exposed to in space. This research will ensure that future female astronauts
are protected as much as possible. Earlier studies were mainly based on
male astronauts and thus failed to consider the needs of women.

All of the Artemis missions will be launched
using NASA's Space Launch System.

INTERNATIONAL PROJECTS

The Apollo missions (pp. 24–29) were motivated more by politics than by science, and as a result they were better funded. Eventually, missions to the Moon just became too expensive, and so they were stopped. Today, many projects are collaborations between several countries, or partnerships with private companies, which lowers the costs for the individual participants.

LUNAR GATEWAY
(Planned space
station in lunar orbit)

LUNAR GATEWAY

The Lunar Gateway is a space station that is planned to remain in lunar orbit. It is designed to serve as a waystation for astronauts headed for the Moon and as a starting point for longer missions to Mars or to asteroids near Earth.

STARSHIP HLS

A modified version of SpaceX's *Starship* rocket is envisioned to ferry future astronauts from lunar orbit to the Moon's surface and back.

STARSHIP HLS
(Proposed lunar
lander from SpaceX)

CHRISTINA H. KOCH

Koch holds the record for the longest space mission by a woman—328 consecutive days. She is also set to become the first woman to orbit the Moon as part of the *Artemis 2* mission in 2025.

DIVERSE CREW

Unlike the Apollo missions, the Artemis missions will be staffed by crew members from many different backgrounds. On the *Artemis 2* mission, the first woman, the first African American and the first Canadian will orbit the Moon. Crews for later Artemis missions will include astronauts from Europe and Japan.

WHO WANTS TO GO TO THE MOON?

In addition to Europe and the USA, other countries are planning missions to the Moon as well. Even now, space probes are preparing the way for future crewed missions.

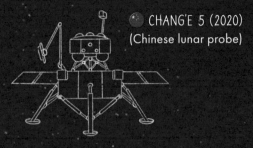

☽ CHANG'E 5 (2020)
(Chinese lunar probe)

The Chinese lunar probe *Chang'e 5* brought back rock samples from the Moon's surface in 2020.

◖ RASHID (2022)
(Emirati lunar rover)

The *Rashid* lunar rover was the first lunar mission launched by the United Arab Emirates. It crashed in 2023 while attempting to land on the Moon.

◉ PRAGYAN (2023)
(Indian lunar rover)

✺ DANURI (2022)
(South Korean lunar orbiter)

Danuri orbits the Moon searching for ice on the surface.

In 2023, the *Pragyan* rover landed on the Moon, while the orbiter *Chandrayaan 3* stayed in lunar orbit.

◉ SLIM (2024)
(Japanese lunar lander)

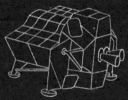

In 2024, Japan became the fifth country to softly land a spacecraft—*SLIM*—on the Moon. *SLIM* stands for *Smart Lander for Investigating Moon*.

SPACE PROBES

Unlike satellites, space probes leave the Earth's orbit to study other objects in space. Space probes consist of up to three parts: orbiter, lander and rover. The **orbiter** stays in orbit, while the **lander** and **rover** land on the surface. There are two types of landing: a **hard landing**, when the probe breaks apart, and a **soft landing**, when it stays intact. The rover is a robotic vehicle that can drive around to study a larger amount of terrain.

Soon people will build a permanent base on the Moon.

The plan is to have a base that will allow people to stay on the Moon's surface for an extended period of time.

That way, the Moon can be studied more closely than ever before.

MOON BASE ON THE SOUTH POLE

In most plans, the base is located on one of the high plateaus around the Shackleton crater on the Moon's south pole. Sunlight never reaches the bottom of the 4-kilometer-/2.5-mile-deep crater, and it's so cold down there that it could have large quantities of frozen water. In contrast, the Sun always shines on the mountain peaks surrounding the crater.

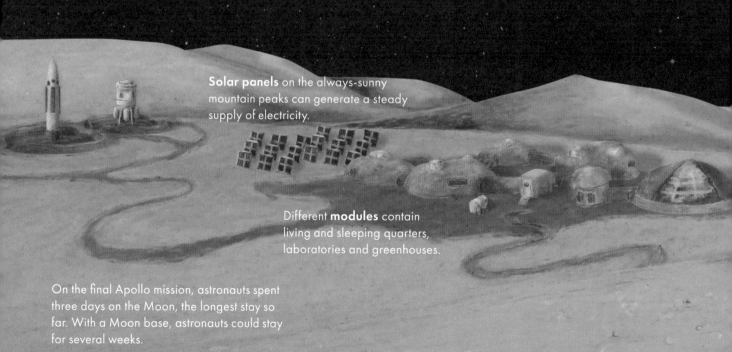

Solar panels on the always-sunny mountain peaks can generate a steady supply of electricity.

Different **modules** contain living and sleeping quarters, laboratories and greenhouses.

On the final Apollo mission, astronauts spent three days on the Moon, the longest stay so far. With a Moon base, astronauts could stay for several weeks.

MOON BASE

Several countries and private companies plan to build a crewed base on the Moon as soon as the early 2030s.

HISTORY WRITTEN IN MOON ROCK

One goal of the Moon missions currently being planned is to more closely study lunar geography and lunar rocks, to learn more about the formation of the Earth and our solar system.

Lunar landers will bring astronauts and supplies from the Lunar Gateway space station to the Moon base.

New **space suits** and **lunar vehicles** are being designed for longer stays on the Moon.

Stories about the Moon have been
told for thousands of years . . .

. . . and now a new story is just beginning.

The story of our journey to Mars.

THE RED PLANET

Like the Moon, our neighboring planet Mars has long been
an object of fascination.

EARTH
MOON

PLANETARY NEIGHBORS

Mars is one of Earth's two neighboring planets, and
they are very similar. A long time ago, Mars, like Earth,
had a dense atmosphere and large quantities of water.
Today, however, Mars is a cold desert and neither liquid
water nor life have been found there so far.

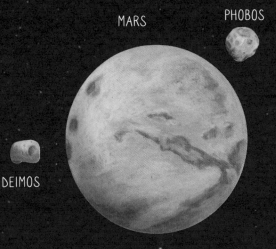

PHOBOS

MARS

DEIMOS

Mars completes a full rotation in
24 hours and 40 minutes. A **Mars
day** is thus only slightly longer than
a day on Earth. But to complete one
revolution around the Sun, Mars takes
687 days—so a **Mars year** is almost
twice as long as an Earth year.

The average
temperature on Mars
is -63°C/-81.4°F.

Olympus Mons is the
tallest mountain and the
largest volcano discovered
in the solar system so far. It is
26 kilometers/16 miles tall.

The line on the right shows you how
far the Moon and Mars are from
Earth in relation to one another.

A LONG JOURNEY

The ISS is located about 400 kilometers/249 miles above Earth. The Moon is an average of
384,000 kilometers/239,000 miles away from Earth. And at its closest proximity to Earth, our
neighboring planet Mars is 60 million kilometers/37 million miles away. If it were possible to
drive to space in a car going 80 kilometers/50 miles per hour, the trip to the ISS would take five
hours. But it would take you six and a half months non-stop to get to the Moon, and more than
85 years to get to Mars. Rockets are much faster than cars, but a trip to Mars and back would
currently still take two to three years.

MARS

TRAVEL TO MARS

A few plans are currently in the works to send the first people to Mars as early as the 2030s.

RED PLANET OR ROBOT PLANET?

In 1997, *Sojourner*, the first Mars rover, landed on the "Red Planet." It was hardly bigger than a microwave. Since then, five more rovers have left their tracks in the red sand. This makes Mars the only planet that is "inhabited" by robots.

During the day, the sky on Mars is orange, but when the Sun sets, it turns dark blue, as can be seen in this photo taken by one of the Mars rovers.

The 50-centimeter-/20-inch-tall *Ingenuity* was the first **helicopter** on Mars. In order to fly in the thin Mars air, its rotor blades had to turn extremely fast.

INGENUITY
(USA, 2021–2024)

Zhurong is the only Mars rover to date that was not built by the United States.

PERSEVERANCE
(USA, 2021–)

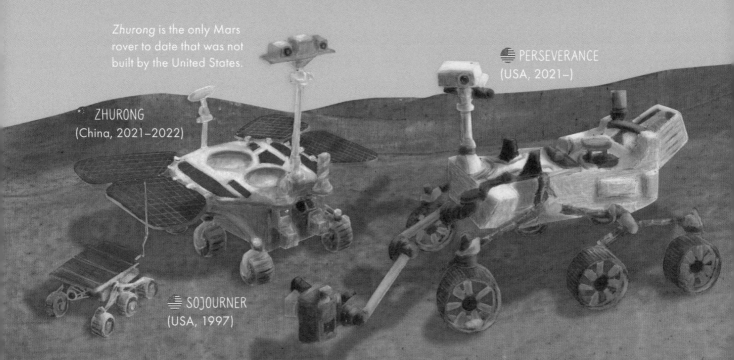

ZHURONG
(China, 2021–2022)

SOJOURNER
(USA, 1997)

The story of humans in space is not yet over . . .

. . . and you could be part of the next chapter.

You could leave your footsteps on the Moon's
dusty surface . . .

. . . or even, one day, in the red sand on Mars.

10 . . . 9 . . . 8 . . . 7 . . .

Are you game?

GLOSSARY

Did you see a word that you didn't understand?

Astronaut: Someone who travels to space (p. 19)

Atmosphere: Protective bubble made of gas that surrounds a planet or moon

Cosmonaut: Russian name for astronaut (p. 19)

Gravity: Strong attractive force that allows large objects like planets to hold onto smaller objects (p. 6)

Lander: Takes astronauts from orbit to the surface of a planet or moon (p. 26)

Lunar lander: see Lander

Lunar rover: see Rover

Lunar probe: see Space probe

Mars rover: see Rover

Module: Part of a space station (e.g. living module)

Orbit: Path that an object in space takes when it flies around another object (p. 15)

Outer Space: Empty space between objects in the universe (p. 11)

Rocket: Takes satellites, space capsules or space stations into space

Rover: Robotic vehicle that studies the surface of a planet or moon

Satellite: Device in Earth's orbit that takes pictures and relays signals

Solar energy: Electricity generated from the Sun

Soviet Union: Former country in Eastern Europe and Asia. Also called the USSR (p. 40)

Space agency: State institution or private company devoted to space exploration

Space capsule: Takes astronauts or supplies into space with the help of a rocket

Space exploration: Study of the universe using astronauts, probes and satellites

Space probe: Spacecraft that leaves Earth's orbit to study other planets and moons (p. 65)

Space station: Scientific laboratory in space (p. 30)

Space suit: Protects astronauts and supplies them with oxygen (p. 27)

Space telescope: Telescope in space (p. 36)

Spacewalk: When astronauts leave their spacecraft and move around in space (p. 23)

Supply capsule: Space capsule that brings supplies to a space station

Taikonaut: Chinese term for astronaut (p. 19)

Telescope: Device used to make distant objects, like planets or moons, appear larger so they can be seen better. See also Space telescope

Universe: Endlessly large space that contains everything there is. Also called the cosmos (p. 11)

USSR: See Soviet Union

Weightlessness: Absence of gravity that causes objects to float freely

Would you like to learn more about one of the topics discussed in this book?

More on the Moon:
The Moon by Hannah Pang and Thomas Hegbrook (Tiger Tales, 2019)

More on space stations:
Behind the Scenes at the Space Stations: Experience Life in Space by Giles Sparrow, Vijay Shah, and Peter Bull (DK Publishing, 2022)

When the ISS and Tiangong can be seen in the sky:
www.astroviewer.net/iss/en/index.php

See a rocket or a space suit in real life:
National Air and Space Museum (Washington, D.C.)
Kennedy Space Center (Cape Canaveral, FL)
Houston Space Center (Houston, TX)

EDUCATOR'S GUIDE

Reflect, Observe and Imagine to continue your own mission!

Reflect

- Have you heard of the "Man in the Moon?" Has anyone said to you, "It must be a full moon" when things seem a little wild or out of control? For thousands of years before telescopes allowed us to see the Moon clearly, people imagined the moon was a spirit or god that kept watch over the people on Earth. Why do you think they believed that? What do we now know about how the Moon's gravitational pull affects life on Earth?

- In the 1950s and 60s, the United States and the former Soviet Union were in a "space race." Each country wanted to be first to get to outer space and land on the Moon. Why do you think the leaders of those countries wanted to be first? Why does exploring outer space and the Moon matter to our life on Earth?

Observe

- How does your view of the Moon change over the course of a month? What about between night and day? Sketch the Moon during the day and at night each day for a month to chart its phases.

- What kind of machines have taken animals, people and satellites to outer space and the Moon? Look at the illustrations of rockets throughout the book and create a chart to compare their heights. Have rockets gotten bigger or smaller over time? Why might that be?

Imagine

- What would it be like to live on a space station for a week? After you read about daily life on the International Space Station (ISS), write a few short journal entries from the perspective of an astronaut. Why is the astronaut on the ISS? What is it like to eat, sleep and work? What do they do in their free time? What is hard about life on the ISS? What is fun? What do they miss about life on Earth?

- Examine the drawing of the Moon's surface on page 10 and think about the variations in its terrain. Then, look at the drawings on pages 62 to 65 of recent lunar rovers and probes that different countries have designed and launched. What do you notice about those designs? Sketch your own design for a rover or probe. What kind of work will your machine do? How will the design help it complete its work?

SHOOT FOR THE STARS!

Download more resources about

Mission Moon

for use in the classroom or at home:

hello.helvetiq.com/missionmoon

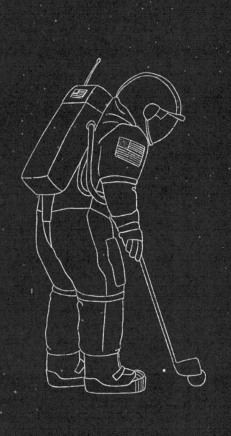